A Day at the Seaside

A Day at the Seaside

San Francisco's Sutro Heights, Cliff House, and Sutro Baths

by Ariel Rubissow Okamoto

GOLDEN GATE NATIONAL PARKS ASSOCIATION

SAN FRANCISCO, CALIFORNIA

The author and the association would like to thank the rangers and volunteers of the National Park Service's Division of Interpretation at Golden Gate National Recreation Area for their interest and assistance. Thanks are also due to individuals and the helpful staff members associated with the regional archives consulted in the course of the photographic research for this publication.

Library of Congress Catalog Card Number 96-78730

ISBN 1-883869-24-2

Editor: Susan Tasaki
Designer: Jamison Spittler
Production Assistant: Diana S. Larrimore

Printed on recycled paper in Hong Kong through Global Interprint, Inc.

Front Cover: Wading on Ocean Beach, with the Cliff House and Seal Rocks in the background, circa 1900; courtesy California Historical Society, San Francisco, Herman S. Hoyt Collection (FN-26335).

Frontis: Stormy seas and big crowds often left Ocean Beach in need of the services of this grooming team; courtesy GGNRA/PARC (Charles Fennel, photographer, P80-076n).

The photographs included in this book are from a variety of San Francisco Bay Area archives as well as individual and family collections. Credits are organized by collection name, with specific inventory information (as available) in parentheses. For further information on any of these photographs, please contact the appropriate source.

Bancroft Library, University of California, Berkeley: pp. 5; 6; 7 (T. E. Hecht, photographer); 8; 9 (Rodolph Collection); 10; 30; 32; 34; 35; 41 (Rodolph Collection)

Marilyn Blaisdell Collection: pp. 3, 13 (W. C. Billington, photographer); 19; 65

California Historical Society, San Francisco: pp. 4 (Piggott, Santa Rosa, photographer, FN-22707); 26 (FN-08729); 29 (R. J. Waters, SF, photographer, FN-12949); 42 (FN-25950); 53 (left, FN-17976); 57 (top, FN-06794; bottom, FN-18538); 59 (FN-12466); 60 (FN-26910); 63 (FN-12572); 70 (left, FN-06848); 73 (FN-18522); 74 (top, FN-18460); 75 (top, FN-18698); 76 (FN-22931)

Cliff House Visitor Center: pp. 1 (courtesy, Robert Holloway); 21; 23 (W. C. Billington, photographer)

Golden Gate National Recreation Area/Park Archives and Records Center (PARC): pp. 2 (76-56); 12 (80-C-47); 14 (I. W. Taber, photographer; P79-246n); 16 (78-182); 17 (top left, 80-20); 20 (top, 80-C-31; bottom, 76-E-60n); 22 (A11.27806nl); 24 (left, P84-119.30nl); 25 (80-35); 28 (78-180); 31 (left, A12.23.472); 33 (76-E-71n); 37 (file no. 1225); 38 (T. E. Hecht, photographer, 80-C-21); 39 (left); 47 (bottom, 80-C-30); 48 (top, 79-C-26; bottom, 80-C-40); 49 (80-C-36); 50 (76-57); 51 (80-57); 52 (P79-247.055); 53 (right, 77-161-16); 54 (Piggott, photographer, 76-64); 56 (P80-028.21); 62 (GOGA 1766.0001, PAM neg. box 16); 64 (80-C-200); 66 (80-62); 67 (top, 78-C-170); 75 (bottom, 86-C-25n); **back cover** (80-17)

Carol Holsworth: p. 36 (left)

National Maritime Museum/San Francisco Maritime National Historic Park: pp. 11 (I.W. Taber, photographer, P84-102.12n); 17 (right, I. W. Taber, photographer, P84-102.4n); 18 (left, I. W. Taber, photographer, P82-102.39n; right, P79-247); 39 (right, P80-037.3); 40 (W. C. Billington, photographer, P84-119.37); 44 (W. C. Billington, photographer, P80-156.5nl); 46 (W. C. Billington, photographer, P84-119.17); 55 (A3.30748n); 61 (W. C. Billington, photographer, P84-119.59)

Henry W. Pearson: p. 36 (right)

San Francisco History Center/San Francisco Public Library: pp. 27; 43; 45; 47 (top, T. E. Hecht, photographer); 58; 67 (bottom); 68; 69; 70 (right); 71; 72; 74 (bottom)

San Francisco's Spirit of Seaside Recreation

Many family albums feature a snapshot of grandma and the kids at the beach; for San Francisco families, there's almost always been a Cliff House in the background (both real and painted, as in this studio backdrop).

Since the first white, wooden Cliff House rose on the city's Pacific Coast cliffs in 1863, San Franciscans have been spending days at the seaside in its shadow — picnicking on the wide sands of Ocean Beach below, strolling among the fine trees and flowerbeds that grew on Sutro Heights up above,

splashing in the saltwater pools of the nearby Sutro Baths, or riding the rollercoasters at Playland-at-the-Beach.

While some of these seaside attractions are long gone, San Franciscans still flock to this wave- and wind-whipped corner of the city, reaffirming the area's nearly century-and-a-half-long role as a recreational retreat for its urban neighbors.

The area's first visitors were Ohlone Indians, who came to fish and hunt in this naturally rich coastal zone; its second, Spanish explorers who named its

major promontory Point Lobos after the barking sea lions; its third, the city's social elite, who could afford the toll road out to the beach and pricey dinner fare at "The Cliff."

The man who would remake this wild corner of the city into a wonderland of parks, pools, and eateries for the masses first saw San Francisco in 1850. Twenty-year-old Prussian-born Adolph Sutro sailed through the Golden Gate on the steamer *California,* searching for his fortune in the gold-rich state.

Though he started with a tobacco business, his reputation and wealth were built upon the tunnel he designed to drain and ventilate the silver mines of Nevada's Comstock Lode. At the time, thirty mines tapped the lode in a confusion of shafts and tunnels filled with hot water, bad air, and steam that reeked like rotten eggs. It took fifteen years for Sutro to raise the money and political will to drive his four-mile-long tunnel through the lode. The increasing temperature proved one of the greatest dif-

ficulties he faced — rising from 72°F at the tunnel entrance to 114°F on the rock face — so hot that Sutro himself eventually stripped off his shirt and joined the work crews to rally them on to the finish. When completed in 1878, the tunnel won acclaim as a world-class engineering feat. At age forty-nine, Sutro returned to San Francisco a millionaire.

He used some of this bounty to acquire twenty-two hundred acres of land around the Cliff House, which by then (1881) was a somewhat disreputable entertainment hall. These sandy acres on San Francisco's western flank included a cottage perched on a rocky promontory overlooking the ocean, previously owned by musical hall proprietor Sam Tetlow.

Sutro planted trees, grass, and flowers around his humble new home; dotted the grounds with European statues; and opened "Sutro Heights" to the public in 1885. He went on to build Sutro Baths, a fabulous, three-acre glass palace.

In the late 1800s, thousands gathered at the San Francisco seaside to see spectacles such as swimming championships, ship-wrecks, tight-rope walks, and this hot-air balloon feat. In 1886, Thomas Baldwin jumped from the balloon a thousand feet above the beach, wearing a new invention called a "parachute."

When Sutro bought the Cliff House (also in 1881), he charged his manager with remaking it into a family-style establishment. After it burned down in 1894, he replaced it with a structure ornamented with the towers and tur-rets of a wooden castle — an opulent building much-loved by the populace. And when this too succumbed to flames, his daughter erected the modern-day Cliff House.

Sutro planted trees all over the city, and served as San Francisco's mayor and a stan-dard-bearer of people's rights from 1893 to 1897. For a while he owned the Ferries and Cliff House Railroad, and waged a campaign against the greed and monopolies of various corporate interests in his city (including the Southern Pacific Railroad, which he called the "Octopus"). He also led a successful crusade to establish a sanctuary for the sea lions and other marine mammals on the rocks below the Cliff House.

Sutro's great love for his seaside home didn't stop him from traveling far and wide. He

explored Australia in search of drought- and salt-tolerant plants for his gardens; bought books from Bavarian monasteries, English dukes, and Palestinian merchants (most of his 100,000 volumes, which once comprised the largest private library in the world, were lost in the 1906 earthquake); and collected "bricabrac" spanning centuries and cultures for the glass cases of his Sutro Baths museum. Despite this busy life of travel and good deeds, he also man-aged to have six children with his wife Leah. Sutro died with more land than money in 1898, but the spirit of seaside culture, natural beauty, and recreation that he kindled remains very much alive on San Francisco's shores today.

Though the baths burned in 1966 and the amusement park on the beach below waned and was finally dismantled in the 1970s, the National Park Service continues to maintain three center-pieces of this seaside recreation area: Ocean Beach, Sutro Heights, and the Cliff House. Indeed, plans are afoot to remove the Cliff House's modern façades and additions, restoring it to its original classic lines, and to build a new visitor center above the ruins of Sutro Baths.

In the meantime, San Franciscans and visitors continue to picnic on the beach, surf the waves, eat at the Cliff House, and walk in the gardens of Sutro Heights and the wilds of the surrounding coastal headlands — snapping new pictures of a day at the seaside for the family album.

A Day at the Seaside

1860s – 1890s

Stepping out for a Sunday jaunt or picnic by the sea wasn't as easy
for San Franciscans of the late 1800s as it is today. Back in those
days, six miles of sand dunes lay between the city's perimeter and
Ocean Beach on the Pacific shore — a landscape locals aptly named
"The Outside Lands." (Photo taken from 33rd Avenue looking east
across today's Richmond District and Golden Gate Park.)

"There was a continual nodding and buzzing from one carriage to another (and) a

Toll gate for the Point Lobos Road out to the Cliff House (pictured here near the former Calvary Cemetery). Built in 1864, this 110-foot-wide road made of broken stone and mineral pitch offered the first easy route across the dunes to the ocean. Indeed the drive became as much a part of a Sunday at the seaside as did the destination. An 1871 tourist guide described the road as the "broadest, hardest, smoothest and longest track in the state. A million dollars worth of legs and wheels flash by a man in a very few hours on this fashionable drive." The road later became Geary Boulevard.

constant succession of spins on the track between the flyers" Captain Junius Foster, Cliff House proprietor

Seaside activities of the 1880s included a stroll on the beach or a picnic in the sand serenaded by barking sea lions and the thundering surf. Those in search of a more comfortable meal could lunch on chicken and lemonade inside the Cliff House.

"Our picnic at the Cliff," according to the Rodolph family album.
At the center of this November 1884 photo sits Francis B. Rodolph,
a well-known Berkeley lawyer.

Relaxing by the seaside was no picnic for ladies of the late 1800s, when fashion dictated that even lounging in the sand required high collars, full skirts, and a feathered or flowered hat, not to mention corsets, bustles, and petticoats.

Sutro Heights' balconies and overlooks made favored spots for clifftop conversation and contemplation.

Seaside visitors brave the narrow suspension bridge across the crash-
ing surf between Sutro Cove and Flag Rock, also known as "Fishing
Rock." The bridge was removed in the 1880s in favor of a more sub-
stantial seawall.

Sutro Heights CULTURE FOR THE MASSES

Adolph Sutro carved a beautiful park out of what one 1886 reporter called the "rocky waste" and "howling wilderness" above the Cliff House. Sutro laid out walkways; planted groves of trees; designed flowerbeds; imported statues; and built a conservatory, parapet, and grand balcony. Sutro Heights (shown above before all the statues were in place) opened its gates to the public in 1885. At right is the circa 1889 plan for the Sutro Heights — Cliff House area.

Seawall

Aquarium

Swimming Pond

Fishing Rock

Terminus of & Cliffhouse

Ocean Terrace

Depot

Ferries Railw

Windmills

← Aquarium

Road to Trout Pond

Trout Pond

Point Lobos Road

Lovers Lane

Shady Path

Cottage

Sheds

Stables

Serpentine Drive

Woodland Walk

3

8

Point

Ivy Lane

20

7

15

Cliff-House

Sheds

Boarding House

17

Maze

Inspiration Point

North Esplanade

13

8

New Drive

Cliff-House Road

South

Shady Lawn

7

6

Palm Avenue

Ocean

14

Parapet

24

9

10

21

2

11

Sandy Beach

Esplanade

Site for proposed Library or Museum

12

Conservatory

23

Drive to Park

South Esplanade

22

Dolce far niente Balcony

OCEAN

gl.Feet

Sutro Heights, San Francisco

Pan 272

"Many a grateful heart, beating beneath a threadbare jacket, has blessed the man who has made all these wonders of art and nature possible of enjoyment without price." SAN FRANCISCO DAILY REPORT, JUNE 18, 1894

"I entered the gate and found myself transported, as it were, from a desert to a paradise. Wending my way along the graveled and flower-bordered walk.... I observed figures on all sides artistically arranged and surrounded with lovely grass lawn studded thickly with trees.... I watched a living fawn grazing the succulent grass as far as the rope he was tied with would permit... saw a reclining statue of a large buck, with his long antlers, suggesting hunter's sport in the mountains... a row of busts upon pedestals of eminent men of the past.... The music from a piano came floating out of an open window in the residence of the proprietor, lending a charm to this bower of beauty." *W.H. Briggs,* *San Francisco Morning Call,* October 16, 1886

In 1884, Sutro imported two hundred plaster sculptures from Belgium to decorate the Heights, seeking to expose bohemian San Franciscans to European culture. The sculptures ranged from Greek goddesses to famous authors, and from lifelike animals to mythic beasts such as the griffin (part eagle, part lion) at right. Hauling the statues across the dunes between the city docks and their new seaside home cost $5 per ton — twice as much as the shipping costs across the Atlantic and around Cape Horn. Once installed, some became popular roosts for peacocks and eagles. Live monkeys, chickens, and fawns also wandered the grounds.

"There is a statue in every piece

f marble, a form of beauty in every barren rock..." ADOLPH SUTRO

It took a staff of ten gardeners, as well as a treeman, roadmaker, gatekeeper, machinist and helper, and coachman and driver to keep Sutro Heights worthy of its reputation as one of the finest private gardens on the Pacific Coast.

Floral tapestries, or *parterres*, were popular in America and England in
Sutro's Victorian times. Heights visitors saw these beds of seasonal and
annual flowers trimmed, tamed, and arranged into amazing shapes.

Sutro continued his tradition of building conservatories later when he constructed a gigantic glass bathhouse — topped with two towers and crammed with potted plants — in a cove below the Heights.

The front of this Sutro Heights conservatory was sheltered by a sculpted, 130-foot-long Gnomas arborvitae hedge. Arborvitae, a popular East Coast conifer, was used in many Victorian-era gardens.

"The view here stirs sluggish blood and enlivens the whole system. To hand, is a luxuriant garden." MORNING CALL, APRIL 20, 1886

Crowning Sutro Heights were a one-story gallery with a Queen Anne tower (photo above, left) and a watertank house and observatory (photo above, right). From 1884 until the 1920s, visitors could purchase postcards and photographic services — the parapet was a favorite site for a souvenir snapshot. The gallery also rented glasses for watching seals.

the west is the ocean, with its stretch of 6,000 miles; the east, right at

A favorite look-out was the Heights' 280-foot, semi-circular parapet topped with thirty stone crenellations. The cannon, a type known as a Parrott gun, was purely ornamental; Sutro may have purchased it as army surplus.

A cantilevered balcony named *Dolce Far Niente*, meaning "sweet to do nothing" in Italian, overhung the southern cliff of the Heights. Below the balcony (left), the ocean and Ocean Beach provided the spectator with an everchanging vista.

The man who created the balconies, avenues, and beauties of Sutro Heights also lived among his treasures. Adolph Sutro, shown here in front of his home, entertained many celebrities in his modest cottage, including President and Mrs. William Henry Harrison, Oscar Wilde, Andrew Carnegie, and Joaquin Miller. He once wrote "These western shores should become the lands of cultured groves and artistic gardens, the home of a powerful and refined race. To reach this happy consummation a taste for the beautiful in nature must be engendered among the masses…"

A Day at the Seaside

early 1900s

Getting to the seaside in the early 1900s meant taking a coach, streetcar, or railroad ride.

Seaside visitors could chose from three different railroads — the scenic Ferries and Cliff House Railroad around Lands End (above), the Sutro Railroad down today's Geary Street (see page 33), and the Park and Ocean Railroad through Golden Gate Park (left). A Sunday seat in the open air coaches of the Ferries and Cliff House Railroad, completed in 1888 and operational until 1906, offered riders thrilling views of the Lands End coastline on their way to the seaside. But landslides plagued the railroad's infancy — tracks were known to slide down the hill at the rate of two inches per day. At the end of the line, Bertie the Birdman's trained canaries entertained riders by loading and firing a little cannon and singing songs.

The ride from the city to the seaside only cost five cents each way, thanks
to a concerted effort by Adolph Sutro to keep fares affordable.
Or, visitors could hire a private touring car (left).

34

Ocean Beach, July 9, 1905

hither by the yellow sands upon which its restless surf breaks ceaselessly."

SAN FRANCISCO DAILY REPORT, JUNE 18, 1894

Seaside visitors could see and be seen, show off their new hats, and inhale the salt air on the Ocean Beach promenade. They might also enjoy a plate of crabs or mussels at the Seal Rock House (two-story white building at left). This establishment, reputedly wrought from the timbers of an 1850s shipwreck, was one of the first saloons built on the San Francisco seaside.

36

Henry Pearson (age one) and his parents Samuel and Elizabeth Pearson came to Sutro Heights all the way from New Zealand in March 1911. Pictured here with a parapet cannon, they made the long and arduous journey to San Francisco for a Methodist convention.

Almost every San Francisco native had a photo capturing a seaside adventure such as this of Guido Aloysius Ghiselli (left, at about 20 years of age) and friends from the Dolphin or Salesian Club (circa 1910). Guido — born in San Francisco's North Beach in 1889 — and his mother and brothers ran the Ghiselli Brothers produce business on Washington Street.

The Three Cliff Houses

SHACKS, SPIRES & COLUMNS

A view of Ocean Beach and the future Sunset District from the Cliff House, 1865

omforts and refinements of civilization from Nature in her rudest aspect..."

Bret Harte

In 1863, real estate tycoon Charles Butler built this first Cliff House on San Francisco's Pacific shore so close to the water that, as one reporter put it, "patrons could pitch a biscuit into the sea from their seats."

From the outside, the first Cliff House looked like a plain, one-story clapboard-and-frame structure, but the inside featured a plush parlor soon filled with well-known, wealthy San Francisco families such as the Stanfords, Crockers, and Hearsts.

By 1868, the first Cliff House had tripled in size with the addition of two wings, a sunning platform, and a seaside balcony. When Adolph Sutro bought it in 1881, the "Cliff's" reputation was somewhat tarnished, and it was up to Sutro and his managers to transform it into a place to attract families.

The first Cliff House in its third and final incarnation. The new owner,
millionaire Adolph Sutro, kicked out the low-life gamblers and women
of ill-repute who had gradually taken it over from the toffs, and repaired
it after a ship exploded on its door step, only to see it burn to the
ground on Christmas Day in 1894.

On January 15, 1887, the little schooner *Parallel* wrecked on the rocks off the Cliff House. Later that night, the forty-two tons of black powder in her hold exploded with a sound that woke the city and a force that destroyed windows, doors, plaster walls, and carriage sheds (pictured here) at the Cliff House. The explosion threw the watchman over a hundred yards and attracted fifty- to one hundred thousand sightseers over the next few days.

Terms used by the press to describe the second Cliff House — completed by Sutro in 1896 for a mere $50,000 — included "an enormous chateau-like confection," a "monstrosity," a "wedding cake," a "gingerbread palace," and an "abomination." But the public flocked to the Victorian wonder.

When Sutro commissioned this Cliff House, he asked architects Emile S. Lemme and C. J. Colley to build him a French chateau-style resort similar to San Diego's famous Hotel del Coronado. They anchored the new building, which rose two hundred feet above the ocean, to the rocks with giant iron rods.

The lower floors included tourist concessions, restaurants, bars, dining rooms, and parlors. The third floor offered twenty private lunch rooms and an art gallery, and the fourth a photo gallery, reception room, and sixteen-foot-wide oceanside verandah.

The new resort attracted thousands of San Franciscans and out-of-town visitors, not to mention celebrities such as James Flood, Mark Twain and Sarah Bernhardt. In the photo at left, Lester Whitman and Eugene Hammond are pictured undertaking one of the first coast-to-coast automobile drives in July 1903, the grand Cliff House in the background.

The second Cliff House

Cliff House manager James Wilkins (at the wheel) leased the Cliff House between 1887 and 1907 from the Sutro family for $700 a month. The only condition was that he run it as a "respectable resort."

"The [second] Cliff House closed with one catastrophic blaze...as if to symbolize the end of an age of Victorian splendor...of spacious times which couldn't have been crowded into the hurried age that followed."
ALBERT TOLF

The September 7, 1907, fire that destroyed the second
Cliff House may have been started by an electrical short.

The fire left the cliff without a house.

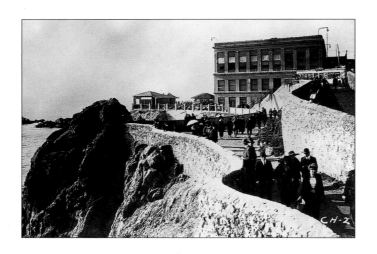

Sutro's daughter, Dr. Emma Merritt, commissioned Reid Brothers, architects of San Francisco's Fairmont Hotel, to design the neo-classical, concrete Cliff House that still stands today. When it opened on July 1, 1909, patrons remarked that "the entire place is fitted up with the utmost good taste" and rejoiced in "the revival of old times." Between 1909 and 1915, several gift shops, a saloon, a candy stand, and this tea house were added.

Photo Cardinell-Vincent Co

Fish Barbecue Cliff House Friday Dec. 8th 1916.

Irene La Cour dances for a Cliff House fish barbecue in 1916.

Between 1937 and 1977, the "Cliff" was owned and remodeled by
George Whitney, proprietor of the popular nearby amusement park,
Playland-at-the-Beach. The new façades he had installed masked the
building's original Classical Revival, Beaux-Arts lines.

A Day at the Seaside

1920s-1960s

Sentimental San Franciscans universally mourn the fun-filled, good old days of Playland-at-the-Beach — opened in the 1920s and torn down in 1972. At this amusement park (shown here in November 1922), kids, teens, and adults alike could turn their insides out by shooting the "Chutes" (a boat and slide combo) or riding the "Big Dipper" roller coaster. The fainter of heart raced bumper cars, rode the merry-go-round, slurped Its-Its ice cream sandwiches, giggled at "Laughing Sal" (now at the Cliff House's Musée Mecanique), practiced rifle shooting, negotiated mirror mazes, or danced and ate 50¢ chicken dinners at Topsy's Roost (entered via a steep slide).

One of the headstones removed from the Laurel Hill and Lincoln Park cemeteries and used for fill to build the Great Highway

Whiling away an afternoon at Ocean Beach also got more comfortable in the 1920s with construction of a seawall and a balustraded "Esplanade" (photo above, right) featuring wide walks and steps for sand-free seaside recreation. The 4,298-foot esplanade reached from the Cliff House to Lincoln Way, flanked by the new 3-mile-long shoreline expressway known as the Great Highway. These projects dramatically altered the natural dune system at the ocean's edge, and completed the transformation of the city's early wilderness of "Outside Lands" into urban neighborhoods and beachfront hardscape.

S.S. OHIOAN ON THE ROCKS
NEAR CLIFF HOUSE — SAN FRANCISCO

Gawkers and relic hunters liked nothing better than a good shipwreck like this of the *Ohioan* in 1936. Between 1850 and 1936,
there were at least fifty maritime accidents off Ocean Beach, where the
surf breaks heavily over a sandbar.

The rescue of Fritz Flukiger from the *Ohioan* on October 8, 1936. The
steel-hulled freighter hit the rocks so hard that sparks lit the night sky.

Dedication of the Sky Tram on May 3, 1955, by local celebrities. From left to right, Dean Maddox (who broadcast a Sunday breakfast radio show from the Cliff House), George Whitney (Cliff House owner) and his daughter Mrs. Floyd Gilman (champagne bottle in hand).

The 25¢ ride on the sky tram took visitors over the pounding Pacific surf from the Cliff House, past the baths, and to Point Lobos between 1955 and 1961.

Eva Whitney takes a ride with three of the 2,000 youngsters who participated in Annual Boys Club Day at Playland on February 3, 1963. Her husband, Playland owner George Whitney, created the event as Boys Club director in the 1930s.

Sutro Baths Swim, Sun & Skate

It took seven years to build the three-acre, steel-and-glass palace that housed Sutro Baths. Completed in 1894, the baths offered six saltwater pools supplied with water by ocean tides and one freshwater plunge bath — all available to swimmers for a mere 25¢ admission.

"Its size impresses visitors at once, yet it is not oppressive owing to

Above the baths lay the "Sutro Pleasure Grounds" where visitors
could ride the Firth Wheel or Haunted Swing (remnants of an 1894
midwinter fair at Golden Gate Park).

he lightness and airiness of the structure." PACIFIC GAS AND ELECTRIC MAGAZINE

In a city with a foggy clime and limited plumbing, a trip to Sutro Baths could be both warming and cleansing — though the rented black wool swimsuits were infamously scratchy. A favorite dare was to plunge first into the hottest and then into the coldest of the seven pools. Bands played on the balconies every Sunday afternoon. On special occasions, swimmers might join in a walking-under-water or trick diving contest, marvel at Jack the diving dog or Professor Karl (who ate and slept underwater), or witness a world swimming championship or a race among soldiers stationed at the Presidio. Up to 30,000 people jammed the place in its heyday (shown here during May Day festivities, 1897).

"All around was the echoing, enveloping sound of splash and laughter and shouts; the close feel of heat and high humidity; the engrossing smell compounded of salt water dampness, wet cloth, human bodies and frying hot dogs." John Allen, *San Francisco Examiner*

The bath house's interior provided a lush environment for its many plants.
In time, one of the palms grew so tall that a hole had to be cut in the floor
above to accomodate its spreading fronds.

This elaborate rococo planter sported busts of Adolph Sutro.

 labels: EGYPTIAN MUSEUM · THE LAST SUPPER · HALL OF MEMORIES · at SUTRO'S NOW! · VICTORIAN ART · SEE INTO NOW · GEMS OF THE WORLD

Swimming was not the only thing to do at Sutro Baths. The upper three
levels of this glass palace had galleries featuring what Adolph Sutro once
called "bricabrac" — objects from around the world that he hoped would
"help install in the minds of youthful visitors a desire for learning..."

Sutro Baths had nine springboards, seven slides, three trapezes, thirty swimming rings, and several high diving platforms; photo circa 1930s.

In the 1930s, Sutro Baths and Jantzen swimwear hosted "Learn to Swim" sessions. At the end of their lessons, the children received diplomas.

In 1934, Sutro's grandson Gustav changed the style of the bath house entrance from ancient Greek to *moderne*. The new "Tropic Beach" featured both a beach and ice rink, as well as volley ball, ping-pong, and dancing.

It took 37,000 watts of power to light this new entrance to Sutro Baths.

Tropic Beach decor, complete with grass huts, table umbrellas, and sandy beach

This 1934 Chevy ad flaunts both wheels and legs.

By the 1950s, the last of the swimming pools had been closed and ice skating received top billing on Sutro Bath's third and final façade.

Skaters Jerry Knudsen, Marie Barrett, and Dorothy Rahe. The rink, home to "The Skating Club" of San Francisco, closed in 1964.

SUTRO'S ICE RINK
C 2758

On merchandise left over 30 days, storage will be charged at the rate of 50¢ per month or fraction thereof. Unless called for within 90 days, you are authorized to sell this merchandise, without notice, for the amount due on same.

Received by
Date
Name
Address
Repairs

PRICE $ NO CHARGE
2758
C
Name
Address
SUTRO'S ICE RINK

This November 13, 1963, five-alarm fire destroyed the gift shop, coffee shop, and hot dog stand adjacent to Sutro Baths.

A four-alarm fire on June 26, 1966, completed the then-ongoing demolition of Sutro Baths. With the fire, San Francisco lost "the closest thing to something out of the Arabian Nights this city has ever seen," according to the local papers, "Xanadu, the Hanging Gardens of Babylon and Madame Toussaint's Wax Museum all rolled into one."

"It is man's labor, and the heroic deeds of men, which put a new and more divine seat to nature's fairest scenes." ADOLPH SUTRO